SUCCESS IN LIFE THROUGH *Revelations*

CHASTINE ROCK

Success in Life through Revelations
©2022, Chastine Rock

ISBN: 978-1-66782-466-6
ISBN eBook: 978-1-66782-467-3

TABLE OF CONTENTS

CHAPTER ONE

"Understanding Ownership"

S uccess in life comes through many forms of applications. Finding
success in every area of life will consist of persistence and dedication.
Because we are believers in Christ Jesus, it is a priority in our life to know how
the Kingdom functions. We have many promises, we have the power of the Holy
Spirit, we have the assistance of angels, the light and sight of the Word, and a High
Priest who ever intercedes for us. These are just some of the benefits that we have
as believers in Christ Jesus, and all of the workings of these benefits come to us
through the Gift of Revelation. Revelations bring light and sight to us. Deuteronomy 29:29, declares that *"the secret things belong unto the Lord our God; but
those things which are revealed belong to us and to our children forever, that we
may do all the words of this law."* We can see from this divine Scripture, that God
has ordained for us to take ownership of what is revealed. That ownership passes
down to our children, so that they also in their generation may benefit from the
light and the sight that revelation brings us. Again, we must understand that
things that are revealed to us are given to take ownership of. It is important to
have this understanding about all the Scriptures, for without taking ownership
you can never really possess something.

Ownership requires us to possess something, regardless of what it is, that
it might be used to benefit our lives and those around us. Ownership of Scripture
simply states that what God has revealed that belongs to me, I must possess it,

not just quote it. Many times, we quote Scripture because it sounds good, it may even feel good to make the confession, and it may be formed out of tradition, just speaking Scripture, but not possessing it. Promises must be possessed in order to own them. Example, you promise your child a certain blessing for cleaning their room. The promise of a blessing inspires the child to clean the room, and then possession of the promise takes place as a reward for the labor of cleaning the room. The promises are never the end of the work, but the blessing is. So, when the child owns the blessing, then the blessing can be used to bring joy to that individual. I hope you got that. It is no different with the promises that God has given to us, for we must take ownership, and not just quote Scripture over and over, thinking that we now have what was promised. Yes confession, and declarations are important based on Scripture, but faith as a possessor, causes us to take ownership of what we are saying, what we are confessing, and what we are making declarations about. Declaring and confessing for a new car is just the beginning of the work to own the car. From many natural illustrations, you and I can see that it is most important to own the Scripture as a possession for ourselves, rather than just speaking about what has been promised. We can look all through the New Testament and how Jesus worked with men and women, that they possessed what they believed for. The Canaanite woman who came for her daughter, her faith caused her to take ownership of that which she desired. Ownership is a powerful tool, for it is the attitude of those who walk by faith and not by sight.

Let's look at an example of taking ownership. In 1 Samuel 17, we have a divine lesson on events that take place when God is about to bring spiritual change. As you read this divine chapter, you note that there are different types of attitudes among the different characters that are displayed in this particular event. There's David's brothers, the Philistine champion Goliath, other soldiers, David, and King Saul. In the atmosphere of the battlefield, Goliath has spoken his mind toward God and His people. As they gave ear to him every day, he drained all of the courage to fight from each and every man and caused them to devalue the cause that was before them. Israel was to be an example to all other nations, as they lived before the Lord and for the Lord. One loud-mouthed, obnoxious giant of a man had silenced all the courage of an entire army. David shows up, and hears what Goliath is saying, and then began to ask what will be done for the man who kills this Philistine giant? The men report that whoever causes this type of victory, (which would have to be out of the ordinary), that man would live as a relative of the king. Almost immediately, someone from David's family speaks up against David's attitude of victory. Seems like there's always somebody that tries to tell you that you can't do what's in your heart to do. David proclaims, *"Is there not a cause?"* What cause was David talking about? David had been through the battle with the lion and the bear, and he had come out owning both of them. David had a lion rug and a bear rug at home to prove his ownership of the fight. David knew that God had caused him to take ownership of that which was greater in strength, greater in fierceness, greater in height, and greater in survival. The lion and the bear represent two of the greatest opponents in the natural, and David had overcome both by the hand of the Lord. After the conversation with King Saul, David enters the battlefield with Goliath. Let's see the difference.

David's statue is not that of a full-grown man, and so Goliath begins to assail on David as he had the armies of Israel. We pick this up in verse 43, where Goliath asked David, *"Am I a dog, that you come to me with sticks?"* Then Goliath began to curse David by his gods. But we noticed in the next verse, how David did not just let Goliath talk, and become an unquestionable listener. An unquestionable listener takes in everything that's being said without questioning the validity of it. Verse 45, is the first time David opens his mouth toward the enemy, and in verse 46, David takes ownership of the victory. You notice how David's confession and declaration is about taking ownership of the victory. He knows that God is with him and all things are working out for his good, so he takes ownership of the victory before contact is made. He then declares that God will get the glory. Why? Because, in his previous battles, David had taken ownership of the victory before the contact ever began. It is no different with you and I today, we must take ownership before we make contact, either with the natural world or the spiritual world. This is why, David could write Psalms 37. He had received revelations that he took ownership of, and he writes to every generation that would follow him. Faith is not foolishness, and certainly foolishness is not faith. Just because you have all the wonderful scriptures in the Bible does not mean that you possess them all. The things that are revealed to you belong to you and to your children, if you take ownership of those things and pass it on. You can pass on a house, land, or anything else to your children less you possess it. In many of the lessons in the Old and New Testaments, we see how important it is to take ownership of a revelation. I pray that as you continue to read through these divine chapters of light and sight, that the Holy Spirit will give revelations to you, that your important walk in the Kingdom of God may have great success.

CHAPTER TWO

"Growing Old in The Lord"

G rowing old can be dangerous, if the principles we live by are not powered by the presence of the Lord. Many of the trails that we travel in life can be treacherous and may contain many pitfalls. However, God has not kept the process of growing older a secret. It's not as if you are blazing the trail as you get older. We certainly have been given many case studies to consider those that have gone on before us. It is not as if no one ever accomplished growing old before us, for many of us have enjoyed the longevity of our parents before us. If growing old catches you by surprise, don't blame God, because He's given us plenty of warning and plenty of advice. If we would look around, we have plenty of opportunity to prepare for growing old in the Lord. The Divine Scriptures show us that wisdom should cause the last chapters of life to be the best chapters of life. Looking at life from an older age, David makes this declaration. Psalms 37:25 says, *"I have been young, and now am old. Yet I have not seen the righteous forsaken, nor his descendants begging bread."* David is looking back at life and how God has blessed him to have a long life. It could be that all of your life has been preparing you for the grand exit. Why? Just look at Job, chapter 42, and view the grand exit of growing old in the Lord. God's oldest have always been among his choicest.

God still remembers the moment we first believed Him, and how the flame of our hearts danced so hot that death couldn't put it out. We were brought forth from death to life, and death could not hinder that decision to walk with Jesus. We must always remember that we are Christians, not perfect beings, but forgiven ones. We hold the sincerity in our heart towards the Lord, regardless of what age we might be bearing in this fallen world. Wherever we are in life, regardless of our age, we are living in a time when God's prophetic word desires to take hold of our days and make them fruitful. Joel 2:25-29, is an invitation into the last days of God's supernatural truths, that will explode upon this earth. In verse 28, we see an invitation for seniors, that's right, for seniors to be involved in the supernatural works of God. This is why, you can never count yourself out just because you've passed a certain age. As I stated earlier, God's oldest have always been amongst His choicest. Sometimes the calamities that are going on around us, cause us to lose our focus on becoming fruitful and maintaining that fruitfulness in the Lord. Sometimes we see seasons of plenty, and as we live longer, we see seasons of scarcity. But this is why, growing old in the Lord is so important, because you can pass on that knowledge to the generation around you. Your conscience and faith provide an avenue of trust in the Lord, regardless of what season it might be. In Genesis 41:30-32, Joseph saw both seasons, the one of plenty and the one of scarcity, as both being under the umbrella of God's jurisdiction. Both were decreed by the Lord. Such revelations give us light and sight into how life may happen for us, even as we grow old in the Lord. So how do we factor in calamities as we grow older? We must first look at what the Bible says, and not what the other sources say. Although calamities are not God's idea, He does forewarn us of the days when calamities may exist. Job 34:10 and James 1:17, are good places to gain revelations. There have been days when my wife and I only had God's character to cling to. The enemy in many forms, comes to attack, and sometimes the battle can be relentless. By the revelations we have of God's goodness, His great character, and His grand faithfulness, is what kept us through each and every encounter. As mentioned before David said, *"he'd grown old from the days of his youth, but he'd not seen the righteous forsaken."*

Why aren't more seniors involved in the supernatural work of God? If you are a senior reading this material for the first time, I pray that you are involved in everything that you can get involved in pertaining to the Kingdom of God. If you are not involved, you are missing a whole world of understanding. You cannot understand things until you get involved, and you cannot use something that you don't understand. Revelation is a byproduct of intimacy with God. As we read in Joel 2:25-29, seniors have been given an invitation to be great dreamers in these days. Dreams come from God in the form of a parable language or illustrated story, which can be filled with symbols, numbers, and even colors. Dreams connect with God's heart, so a dreamers' ability to receive revelation with clarity is connected to the purity of their lifestyle, and to the obedience of what God says. So, the invitation that God is giving us as seniors in this prophetic time, represents a written request for us to do something or make a particular outcome likely. God didn't leave out seniors for His end time work, but declared through His written word, (which is a memorial...something not to be forgotten), that seniors are to be involved in His holy work continuously.

Here is an example of a senior involved in the work of God. Luke 2:25- 40, gives us the divine picture of a senior that is still full of fire, full of light and sight, trusting in the Lord. His name is Simeon, and he's been given a promise, and he's taken ownership of that promise. He's been promised that he would not see death until he had seen God's salvation in Israel. His ownership of the promise, even in his old age, put death on hold. Death could not hinder the promise from happening, and so Simeon waited. That's powerful! A lesson in a lesson, if God declares something to you and you take ownership of it, nothing can hinder it from happening in your life. Why aren't more seniors involved in God's supernatural work? Some become too busy, even to be thankful. Some are against being joyful about God's blessing on their life, because of associations. Some seniors are too prideful and arrogant to be grateful, because that would admit that they are needy. There are many other reasons why many seniors are not involved in God's supernatural work, but that will not excuse them. For God has called **all** to be fruitful, not just buds, not just blossoms, but fruitful.

Philemon 9-10, shares a picture of Paul, the aged, interceding for a loved one that he deems as profitable for the Kingdom of God. Notice Paul declares himself as being old in the Lord, and still involved in the work of the Kingdom. Even in his declaration of himself being older, he is still recognizing the importance of getting others involved in God's supernatural work. It is a powerful thing to have such longevity in the Lord, and to use the experiences of life to guide others into places that they may never get to without your help. God promises us, according to Romans 8:28, to render beauty out of all things, not each thing. Here is an example, when you sip on a cup of coffee and say this is good, what are you really saying? Are you saying that the plastic bag that contains the coffee is good? Are you saying that the beans are good? Or maybe you're just saying the hot water is good? No, no, no. Good happens when **all** of the ingredients work together. Your wisdom, experiences, understandings, gifts, and services all work together to make good happens. God uses "all" of our life to bring things about that are good. Who better knows what life can bring than one who has grown old in the Lord? You can certainly answer that for yourself. God never promised that life would be painless, or that disappointments would be short, but He has promised "never *to leave us nor forsake us*". Grab the revelation that comes from Malachi 3:16, as you are growing older in the Lord.

CHAPTER THREE

"The Revelation of Agreement"

T he revelation of agreement, according to Scripture, says that *"anything you believe, you must become one with"*. When you do, there is a concentration of power ready to be released. If this revelation is not established in your life, it will be impossible to live victorious according to Kingdom principles. Why is it so important to understand this revelation? Because, it involves availability. Let's look at Amos 3:3, scripture poses the question, *"Can two walk together, except they be agreed"*? We see the first part of the question pertains to availability, while the second part of the question pertains to knowledge. In the first part of the question, it relates to a physical faith. Going in the same direction, having the same patience, enduring the same terrain, and not leaving the other behind, are all contained in walking together. In the second part of the question, it relates to the thought life of faith. The spirit of faith creates a voice according to 2 Corinthians 4:13, which gives understanding of our commission, victory, and fellowship. As Scripture stated to us, *"a house divided against itself will never stand"*. In the revelation of agreement, we find that there must be availability to advance to success.

If you notice that upon visiting a fast food chain, they always ask what sauce you would like with your meal. I suggest the "Sauce of Hunger", when you are about to feed on the Word of God. Add hunger to your meal, and the Word will taste much better each time you feed. I give you three ingredients that are incorporated within the Sauce of Hunger. Number one is "desire". Desire is a strong feeling of wanting something, which usually works out through three dimensions. Our "hearts' desire" (Romans 7:22), our "souls' desire" (Romans 12:2), and our "body's desire" (Galatians 5:16). The second ingredient in the Sauce of Hunger, is "decision". Decisions are conclusions that are reached after considerations. These are usually brought forth in two levels, "general decisions" (Psalms 23), and "specific decisions" (Psalms 118:25). Decisions of value and quality become the bits in our mouth, that transform lives. The third ingredient in the Sauce of Hunger is "determination". Determination is the process of establishing something exactly the way it should be. There is only one level of the determination, and that is straightforward. The enemies of our Kingdom know that spiritual growth by any believer cannot be taken for granted, so anything that can be done to hinder your focus on revelation knowledge will be presented to you.

Your alignment in spiritual things pertaining to the Kingdom of God, will shift territories and regions into a Kingdom expression. Your alignment which is agreement, which causes availability, will connect you to the agendas of God's will, that will cause authority through prayer, activity and function, to prevail and bring forth success in every area of life. Acts 10:38, declares that *"Jesus went about doing good, healing all who were oppressed of the devil, for God was with him."* The revelation of agreement puts us in a place where you cannot be ignored by your enemy. He knows that the availability of God's power is with you now because, you are walking in agreement. He understands that every form of wisdom, encouragement, giftings, and miracles, are at your disposal through the revelation of agreement. This is why, he tries to get you to focus on other things that will carry you away from the agreement of walking with God. When you know; that you know; that your words cause a spiritual shift, you would be very careful of what you say. The spirit of faith is always advancing toward the enemy, never backing down. We are as bold as a lion because of our attitude willed to us by our Lord. If you study the life of Joseph in the book of Genesis, you come away with this assessment, Joseph began and ended his crisis with references to God. God was before the famine and God will be after the famine. Why? Because, Joseph walked with God wherever he was in the spirit of faith. Do you recite your woes more naturally than you do heavens blessings upon you? Are you assuming that God is not available? Are you describing the economy or your cranky spouse as being detrimental to your life, and God is not around to help? Remember, *"the things that are revealed to you belong to you and your children, that you may do the law of God."* When you agree and take ownership of those revealed things, you can evict the thoughts of anger that may present themselves through disappointments.

Genesis 26:1 says, that there was a famine in the land. This is nothing new, because famine had existed before. People perish in times of famine, because there is no vision to carry them to provision. That vision comes through the Word of God, which gives light and sight. In verse 12, it says that *"Isaac sowed seed and received in the same year a hundredfold; and the Lord blessed him."* Isaac walked in agreement with God, which caused the availability of God's presence wherever he was. As we said in the beginning of this chapter, if I agree with something, I must become one with it. When we become one with the Lord, as in the new birth, the availability of the Lord's presence is always with us. Study John 14:23, to gain more light and sight. As Isaac walked in agreement with the Lord, a progressive concentration of power was available to be released at whatever he set his hands to do. In sowing seed in a time of famine, we see that Isaac was walking in faith and speaking in faith. His walk was on ground that was not producing for others, and his talk was from the spirit of faith, which advances toward any enemy, and in this case, the lack of resources. As soon as faith speaks, it acts. Again, as soon the spirit of faith speaks, we act. Why? Because, we become one with what we believe. Isaac knew that seed always alters the surface. Isaac knew that sowing his seed along with the concentration of God's multiplying power, that the barren ground would soon produce a tremendous harvest. Well, it did, for he received a hundredfold in that year. This is why, it is so important to have revelation knowledge. It advances you beyond the enemies work in the natural realm and transforms barren territories into Kingdom reservoirs.

Jesus declared in Matthew 16:18, *"that revelation knowledge would build his church, and the gates of hell would have no grip to withstand it."* God's sovereignty doesn't negate our responsibility, it empowers it. Why? Because, when we trust the Lord, we think more clearly and react more decisively. The availability of heaven's resources rest in the hands of the believer who walk in the power of alignment and will speak forth words of agreement from God's table of contents for life. Be delivered, as I call you blessed of the Lord. Go to the Word that covers any situation you might be facing. Keep it before your eyes, ears, your heart and mouth. Go to God on the basis of His provision, not your needs. He already knows you have the need, but do you have the heart to move that mountain. Always know this, you may not have a seat in the house of Congress, but you are seated with Christ Jesus, and that makes a world of difference.

CHAPTER FOUR

"The Revelation of Potential"

In discovering the many revelations throughout Scripture, we embrace the power that can undo what has been done, and reverse that which seems irreversible. As we embrace this revelation of potential, we will embrace the faith of Father Abraham that is recorded in Romans chapter 4. We will first get an understanding of who this revelation of potential is provided for. 1 John 5:1-5 says, *"that we are designed by faith, born of God, unto God, and for God."* Why? To repel and to conquer this natural world and any demonic forces within it. From our spiritual birth we have been equipped with the potential of living as world overcomers in every situation or challenge. It is a common privilege of every born-again believer to live by righteousness. We learned from Scripture that the grace of God is the same yesterday, today, and forever. So, while God has a church in the world, there is the fountain of power that is inexhaustible to every believer. For with God all things are possible. The only condition that is listed in the Word of God for us to take advantage of the privilege of such power is that we must "believe". The doorway to this inexhaustible power can only be open through divine revelation. As Jesus said, *"the gates of hell shall not prevail against His church"*. That church which operates in divine revelation, will open up the doors of potential to every believer within that congregation. For God is no respecter of persons, but He does respect faith. The revelation that Abraham received was of the Lord Jesus Christ coming into the earth, and the revelation that you and I operate by is that Christ Jesus has already come. Neither revelation nullifies the other, and so each revelation from Abraham's day will also bear witness with every revelation of our day. *"For the just shall live by faith, and that faith starts where the will of God is known."* Our spiritual birth has brought us forth to believe on Him that raised Jesus from the dead, not only do we believe in His power, but we depend upon His grace to enter into these great potentials. May the gift of understanding open up to you now the great "Revelation of Potential".

We use our faith to pull into place the real treasures that belong to us. Those deep hopes that you have are not foolish wishes. They are real potentials because of the "anointing of might" that resides inside of you, for it is that anointing that can birth them into your life. Only when you have encounters with the "Spirit of Might", are we empowered to look, and then look again. We keep on looking, because we know through expectation and faith, that we see beyond the natural realm. We see the things that can only be done from a supernatural standpoint. In Ephesians 3:20, a presentation from the laws of power are given to us. It states, *"that God can do exceedingly abundantly above all that we ask or think."* In other words, God goes deeper to give better than what we've asked. Why? Because of His unlimited ability. Numbers 23:19 states, *23:19 states, "that God is not a man that He should lie, nor the son of man that He should repent".* God, not being a man but Spirit, reveals from the Scripture that natural restrictions cannot be put on Him, because He is without limits. So, to walk in the revelation of potential, we must never lose sight of His supernatural origin. Outside of the supernatural, God cannot be defined. So, He is always above reason, and always above the limitations of our wisdom, culture, and even our surroundings regardless of the season of life. Our potential rests on the foundation of God's unlimited ability and resources.

Unbelief is at the bottom of all of our staggering's with the promises of God. It is never the promise that fails, but our faith that staggers at the goodness of those promises. Some people still today have a problem believing that the Lord God is as good as people say He is. Some still struggle in faith, not realizing that the Father sent Jesus to redeem us to his first intent. Walking in divine potential must be experienced, not just spoken about, to lay foundations of faith that others can follow. Psalms 119:1-3 says this, *"Blessed are the undefiled in the way, who walk in the law of the Lord. Blessed are they that keep his testimonies, and that seek him with the whole heart. They also do no iniquity; they walk in his ways."* In other words, as we would put it today, you can't show the way, until you know the way. It is vitally important as a believer, that we talk the talk, and walk the walk, because Jesus is the way, the truth, and the life. So how do we live like Abraham lived before the Lord? How do we walk in that potential that changes our bodies, even as his body was changed? How do we stagger not at the promises, when everything around us seems to be going in the opposite direction? As I said in one of the previous chapters, we may not have a seat in Congress, but we do have one with Christ Jesus. Now let's answer those questions.

Ephesians 2:4-6 says this, *"But God, who is rich in mercy, for his great love wherewith he loved us, even when we were dead in sins, hath quickened us together with Christ, by grace you are saved; and have raised us up together, and made us sit together in heavenly places in Christ Jesus."* Here's the answer that Scripture reveals to us. First, we must renew our perspective of ourselves. We must see ourselves as He sees us and fix our minds on Him. We base our life on this position, rather than our experiences of life. When we focus our minds on Him, He reveals to us more and more about who we really are in Him. The second thing we must do, is to release old patterns of thinking. Release your past, your old self, your old baggage, and your old citizenship. You must die to the past, otherwise, you will never be able to see your future. We take up our cross and die daily. Our bodies hang upon the cross, and even though we live long, our bodies are dying daily to this world. The third thing that we must do, is to remember your purpose. Everyone has a purpose, and even though some never search to find that purpose, purpose was ordained to them before birth, read Psalms 139. Now let's get back to, remembering your purpose. Our goal as a believer, is to participate in God's redemptive plan for the world. You can only understand things when you participate in them. If you have never played football, but only watch as a fan, you never know all the training, exercises, and planning that goes into a football game. Only when you are participating on the field, not in the grandstand, can you understand the physical impact that the game has on your body. So, when we participate in God's redemptive plan, you begin to embrace purpose, as purpose embraces you. Then the revelation of potential begins to unfold, and you know without a shadow of a doubt that you have been born of God, unto God and for God, to repel and conquer this natural world.

CHAPTER FIVE

"The Revelation of Potential"
Part 2

Jesus made various statements about their ability to hear and see. In Matthew 13:14, Jesus said that the ability to see and perceive was critical to possessing the things that you want in life. Through the Spirit of Might, we received the potential again to look and see with expectation and with faith. Through the session on the revelation of potential, I pray that you will gain enough understanding of this revelation to break through your drought, and to come into your wealthy place. In Isaiah 11:2, Scripture says, *"that through the Spirit of Might vision is restored to the visionless and the hopeless."* Through the Spirit of Might, we get a light and sight, as well as the possession of that which we seek. When you turn the light on in a dark room, you not only get the light, but the sight to possess that for which you entered the room for. That's just an example to help you to understand the possibilities of walking in the Spirit of Might. As you renew your perspective of who you are, release old thought patterns, and remember your purpose as a believer, more supernatural authority will be released to you through the wisdom of God. As you press through in these revelations, the awesome power of God in the Spirit of Might (force, valor, and victory) will cause your vision to become a Kingdom vision, and your faith will take its stand as a world overcomer. Don't forget that we are designed by faith, born of God, unto God, and for God. Our exercising Kingdom advancement is to repel and conquer this natural world, and any demonic forces that challenges us.

A great lesson from the Old Testament on the importance of being able to see, is given in 1 Kings 18:42-44. Here lies the process of keep on looking until you see what you desire to see, not what others tell you that they see, or what this world tells you that you should see. The servant was commanded to look, go see. There was a need to go and look again. Sometimes, in prayer we need to keep looking until we see what we are believing for. Elijah's prayer caused a hand sized cloud to appear. That hand sized cloud broke the famine and caused Reformation in Israel. The power to see what others can't see can change the lives of many generations. Elijah was not detoured by the times when his servant said, "he didn't see anything". You can't be detoured either. It is this type of faith that allows us to see the big thing within the little thing. Elijah's faith only needed to see a little cloud, because a mustard seed can grow into a big tree. When you believe for that which is impossible, to accomplish in your own physical strength, keep your faith strong so that it may lay hold of a little part of what you desire. Elijah needed more than just a little cloud to break the power of the drought, just like you need more than $100 to break the power of poverty. But, being able to see a little cloud, opened up the door for him to see the downpours that would solve his problem. You must be able to see the big that can come out of the little in order to break whatever bondage you might be under. Many people make the mistake of trying to see the whole picture before they can see the first scenes. Zechariah 4:10, is another witness to the very Scriptures that we are reviewing.

Jesus' platform is listed in Luke 4:18-19. He states that, *"he is come to bring forth the recovery of sight to the blind, which comes through the Spirit of Might."* The Spirit of Might produces force, valor and victory. So, we see that part of Jesus' purpose was to help us see, because the ability to see is crucial to getting from God. "Force" is the ability to act against, to bring forth resistance. "Valor" is strength to encounter danger with firmness. "Victory" is to overcome the odds or difficulties regardless of the situation. Throughout His ministry, Jesus lived like this everyday, in every place He visited. In John 9:1, is a picture of Jesus exercising the Spirit of Might. At the end of the story, verse 25, the man who was blind but now sees, made the statement. One thing I know, I was blind but now I see. He could only make that statement after being under the power of the Spirit of Might. This is why, it is important to walk with God. He causes us to see and conceive dreams from His heart. We began to become attached to that which we are seeing through faith, and even though it is ahead of us, we connect to it through the Spirit of Might. Like David, we use our faith to pull that which is ahead of us into the present time with us. David got a revelation of God wanting all mankind to worship him in spirit and in truth, and David reached into the future and connected to praise and worship. He then pulled it back into his present day and set up praise and worship to honor God continuously. So, as a believer, as you walk with the Lord, certain things are revealed to you from the unseen world, from that world where everything originates. What you see in that unseen world, you are able to manifest into the seen realm by exercising your faith to pull it into your present time. Now you are probably wondering, why isn't everyone enjoying the revelation of potential? There are many answers to that question, but one of the priority answers is that people are too lazy to study for themselves. I did not say everyone, but there are many professing Christians who do not know why they are professing what they profess. The grace of God is a gift from God to help us live a righteous life, but there are mixed messages of grace that are causing people to miss out on the blessings of what grace provides for us. In John 16:12-13, Jesus reveals that the Holy Spirit would help us to receive as we have the capacity to receive. The capacity to receive is based on the sauce of hunger. How much sauce of hunger do people add to the Word when they study? How much sauce of hunger do people add to the Word of God when they are searching for answers? The Holy Spirit is not a waster, and so if the capacity is not built to hold certain things from the spirit realm, then the individual is not going to receive things that are greater than his capacity.

The verdict of the cross, is the judgment that stands today, as well as it was in the day that it was given. When Jesus died on the cross, a verdict was rendered against the devil and the powers of darkness. Every legal right the enemy held over mankind was abolished. That's right, it was abolished. The Holy Spirit who helps, convinces, and reveals these revelations to us, it is by his ability that we are empowered to see these realities. The result of these realities, breakthrough and full manifestation of restoration in our lives. Not just for us, but for our children and the generations around us. That verdict rendered in Jesus' death, new history began, a new world began, that we might know the things that are freely given to us of God as Scripture says in 1 Corinthians 2:12-16. We now live with the mind free of condemnation, a mind of release, and the mind of blessing. Deep in the mind of God, the Holy Spirit shares with us the things that are freely given of God, that we might have the mind of Christ, and because we believe as Christ believes, therefore we speak what the Holy Spirit teaches us. Use the revelation of potential to see what you have not seen before that you may venture into life we have never ventured before. I call you blessed.

CHAPTER SIX

"The Revelation of Divine Communication"

O ne of the most dynamic truths for the New Testament believer to understand, is the power of the rent veil by Jesus' blood, that now gives us the privilege to hear His voice in our spirits. He tore the curtain in the temple, from top to bottom, he tore the veil in the temple, that all may have access. Access to what? We all now have access to hear His voice in our spirits. That's right, to hear His voice in your spirit no matter where you are. That's how important it is for God to communicate with us. He rent the veil in the temple, that we would have access to enter into God's presence, to talk, as well as listen. Divine communication is all about our ears being open to hear privileged information. As with intimate friends, both talk and both listen, when engaged in communication. From the time you were born again, born from above, every child of God is privileged by the blood of Jesus to enter the holiest of all. From the youngest to the oldest, God's grace permits all to come in, to sit down in His divine presence, to be still and listen to privileged information.

The fastest seed to grow in the Kingdom, is prayer. In Luke 18:1-8, it gives us divine access into God's presence. Jesus' command to us is, *"that man ought to always pray and not faint"* Jesus knows from experience that prayer releases authority, and that authority can change all things. Let's take in a definition of divine communication. It is the gift of language to communicate to the super-natural authority of the universe (Isaiah 43:10-13). As we inhale heaven's will (The Word of God), we exhale God's authority. Jesus knew that prayer done the right way, would bring God on the scene, to bring us out, or to bring us through. Much is gained immediately when we speak God's will in prayer. Yes, He knows that we have needs, and He knows before we get there what we are going to say. We should be in agreement with Him, by speaking His Word back to Him. Good friends always know what the other speaks. If good friends know how their friends talk, we the Sons of God should know how our Father talks. Jesus said to pray, that your situation might be before the righteous judge, who judges rightly. Jesus also knew from experience, that prayer allows you to become a channel for God's will. In Mark 9:28-29, the disciples asked Jesus why were they not an open channel for God's hand to work? Jesus replied to them, prayer and fasting, both create a channel for God's will to flow through you. Everyone desires to be a channel for God's flowing hand, so divine communication is most important. Fasting and prayer are both hot wires in communicating Kingdom privileges. Prayer, being a spiritual work, is an expression of desire on our part. Desire to receive God's will, and to see that will expressed in the earth. Prayer, being a spiritual work, rearranges spiritual territory. Prayer gives us the power to tread on serpents and scorpions through the name of Jesus. Prayer, being a spiritual work, causes families to be set free from iniquitous patterns and old paradigms. From the divine life and pattern the Jesus lived before us, we see from Scripture that Jesus prayed before he ate, he prayed for children and the sick. We also see from Scripture that no one, absolutely no one, ever left a prayer that Jesus prayed, without being satisfied.

Through the Spirit of Faith, we speak that which we believe, which is the Word of God. When we inhale heaven's will and exhale God's authority, divine communication between heaven and earth begin to change circumstances. In Luke 11:1, Jesus is asked to teach His disciples to pray. You notice that none rejected being taught how to pray. They could have asked for instructions on other topics such as public speaking, food multiplication, the true weather fore-cast, or even how to vacate cemeteries. But they didn't. Why were they so enthu-siastically asking Jesus to teach them to pray? It could have been the eye-popping promises that Jesus told them that was attached to prayer. It could have been the experiences they had with Jesus healing all who came to Him. It could have been all the times they heard demons crying out, being afraid of Jesus' power. Something triggered the desire in them to want to pray the way Jesus prayed. Matthew 7:7-8 and Matthew 21:22 are two powerful promises given to those who would pray. The disciples no doubt heard Jesus speak many things about prayer that we do not have, but what we do have, we can use it to change things. Scripture teaches us that there are many people who signed up for Prayer 101, from Genesis to Revelation, men and women have prayed and received through the power of prayer. The disciples walking with Jesus had never heard Jesus attach such power to any other endeavors, except prayer. From Scripture, we do not see that Jesus said plan, and it will be given to you. We do not see that Jesus said you will get anything you work for. We also do not see this phrase written that people use for excuse, "Well the Lord knows my heart". John 15:7 and John 16:23-24 gives us instructions to come before Him with his words, that we might change things. Jesus could only give these stunning promises of prayer by being an example of the power that comes from prayer in manifestation.

"How Not to Pray"

Scripture also tells us how not to pray, because all is open and seen in the spirit realm. The words that you speak are very important, but they can bring life or death. Let's take a closer look. Matthew 6:5 says, *"And when thou prayest, thou shall not be as the hypocrites are; for they love to pray standing in the synagogues and in the corner of the streets, that they may be seen of men. Verily I say unto you, they have their reward."* These were like theater prayers, rehearsed prayers, that nauseated Jesus. Matthew 6:7-8, is running neck and neck with the theater prayers. Jesus says here, *"but when you pray, use not vain repetitions, as the heathen do; for they think that they shall be heard for their much speaking."* In other words, don't try to emulate religious people who don't know God, who say all kinds of vain things without the knowledge of truth. Jesus stunned the audience when He spoke, because He got to the heart of the matter, which made things right. That's just the way truth is. Jesus stunned the farmers, the stonemasons, the cooks, the fishermen, and any other profession within any culture by this next statement of His. In Matthew 6:6, it shows us that Jesus is low on fancy, but high on accessibility. He says this to His audience, *"But when thou prayest, enter into thy closet, and when thou has shut thy door, pray to thy Father which is in secret; and thy Father which seeth in secret shall reward thee openly".* Jesus was saying that prayer, divine communication, can be done anywhere that a heart-felt conversation exists.

"Dealing with It"

"It troubles you; it hurts you; it wears you out; and you can't take it anymore." It seems to be trouble in many ways. Many statements are made because of the trouble that it brings. In 1 Peter 5:7, it tells us *"to put it in the hands of the one who can handle it."* Mary, the mother of Jesus, knew some things about Jesus that others didn't know. She put the continued joy of the wedding feast into Jesus' hands. Her command to the servants were, "do whatever He tells you to do". She knew anxiety free living comes from prayer, because sometimes the challenge is greater than our strength. We need strength that comes from above more so than that which comes from below. In prayer, divine communication, we see there is no distance, or place that God cannot hear from. Just ask Jonah, who made his bed in the belly of a whale. Even from the depths of the sea and the decaying parts in a whale's belly, God can hear. If it is a prayer for correction, or prayer for joy to be established, God hears all (Jonah 2:1-10). Remember what Jesus said in our beginning background Scripture, *"prayer releases authority that changes things"*.

Because divine communication is the gift of language to communicate to the supernatural authority of the universe, that being God, Jesus reveals in Luke 18:7-8, that Daddy God is waiting for men to pray. His will awaits the prayers of men. Why? Because, His will is always in search of a way out for you, or a way in for you.

2 Chronicles 16:9 says, *"that His will is searching for someone to be an expression of His person."* In other words, God is apprehending people to release His grace of Jubilee in their lives. You might be thinking right now about your needs, or someone else's needs. This is why, it is important to follow the Word of God, and never underclaim the promises of God. He is looking for someone that He can show Himself strong through. That just might be you today.

CHAPTER SEVEN

"The Revelation of Divine Authority"

A s you have gotten this far in reading on the success that we have through revelations, it is important for you to realize the unlimited authority in Christ Jesus. Divine authority has been delegated to us that God's will might be set forth in the earth. As we read further in this divine chapter, prepare yourself to speak boldly with authority, and give no room to hesitations or disputes about your God-given rights. Divine authority is given to one delegated, to speak to all worlds, (calling those things which be not as though they are) under the servanthood to the bearer of such authority. We can walk from this picture given in Genesis 1:1-2, with some knowledge of how great divine authority is. Chaos was the present picture, but God said what He wanted, instead of what He had. God continued to say what He wanted, up to 10 times, until He saw what He wanted. So, we see that calling those things which be not as though they were until they are, as a principle of changing things. As we walk in divine authority, we are bearing great authority to confront and change natural and supernatural conditions.

"Then the Fall"

In Genesis 3, it reveals to us that Adam and Eve had a falling out with God, and with each other. Nature fell out of whack, and each individual world of creatures followed suit. The human body became imbalanced, as sin open the door for interlopers to come in. An interloper is a person who becomes involved in a place or situation where they are not wanted or are considered not to belong. All these things came when Adam committed high treason against God. His one sin, disobedience, opened the door for all human life to receive the same judgment for his one offense. Sickness and disease are interlopers, consequences of the same rebellion. All that is happening in the world today that is wrong, came through this rebellion. Adam's sin was disobedience. The thing that he committed was therefore evil, because it was forbidden, and it opened the door for other sins. We can see that the poison from the sin of disobedience is very strong and continually spreading. I named this a spreading sin many years ago, because we can see what it is doing to the human race. By Adam's sin, many are made sinners. Romans 5:17-21, imprints this picture into our renewed mind of just how damaging the spreading sin has become. It declares that we were made sinners. Nothing we could do about it, no generation could change it, and death became the sentence that all mankind would lie under. Who would have ever thought in the past generations that there would be so much sin and evil as there is today? This is why, man must be made over, from the rebirth and even unto receiving a glorified body, because all have been made sinners.

In like manner, by the righteousness and obedience of one, that being Jesus, many are made righteous. This is the power of the gift of grace, the free gift that comes upon all who believes that, *"God so loved the world, that he gave his only begotten son Jesus"*. The obedience of Jesus bought this righteousness in play for us. The disobedience of the first Adam ruined us, but the obedience of the second Adam saves us to the uttermost. Jesus, through his obedience, brought out a righteousness for us and satisfied God's justice. This free gift is unto justification, as by Jesus' resurrection, and ascension, we have been freed from death and entitled to eternal life. We see by the Scriptures from Romans 5:17-21 that the communication of God's grace and love to us through the hands of Christ Jesus, goes beyond the communication of guilt and wrath by the first Adam. We can see by this great picture that God is rather inclined to show great mercy rather than punishment. The poison that Adam gave us through disobedience, has been healed by a stronger antidote, we call it the Blood of Jesus! By Adam's sin, death reigned over all humanity, but by Christ's righteousness, all believers are preferred to reign in life. We have been instated into greater privileges through Christ Jesus and His righteousness, than what we lost by the first Adam's offense. So just from reading these Scriptures, we can see that sin has had its bloody reign unto death, but grace reigns in life and eternal life, through the righteousness of Christ Jesus our Lord. This is where and how divine authority rises from. This is why you and I can walk in the revealed knowledge that Jesus walked in. Jesus was never under the law of sin and death, and He reigned in life over every situation and circumstance. As we look at some of the Scriptures of authority in action, let us bring ourselves to the life of the bearer of such authority. Sin cannot condemn us, disease cannot destroy us, guilt has taken a bloodbath, and death has lost its sting. Now under the righteousness of Christ Jesus, all these have become a showcase of God's grace and power, a demonstration of His ability to redeem. *"Who the Son sets free, is free indeed."*

In Mark 4:35-41, we see the second Adam in full form, not walking under the law of sin and death, but walking under the law of the Spirit of life. He rebuked the wind and told the sea to be still. He wasn't looking at what He had and settling for it as the disciples were. He looked at the sea, the winds blowing, the boat rocking, and His disciples crying out for help, and He gave attention only to what He wanted. If you have ever been out to sea and the winds blow tremendously hard, then you know you are in for a rough ride. The air currents and the tides were both challenging the disciples' faith. Just like everyone else who takes their eye away from faith, things that could be simply solved become complaints. The disciples complained to Jesus as if He didn't care about their safety. Wow! Let me give you a pointer while we are right here. You might want to underline this. What you do right now in a situation, sets the stage for what God does next. Again, to walk in divine authority, you must take responsibility for what you can do, so that God can do what you cannot do. Our faith will require us to *"call things that be not as though they were, until they are"*. When resources are low, you must speak to your business, or paycheck, or other incomes, and instruct them to multiply. Speak restitution and reimbursement, speak paybacks and higher raises, but never sit there and say I'm busted and disgusted. Your authority carries through the spiritual realm, and contacts are waiting to connect to your words.

1 Corinthians 10:21, reveals to us that duality causes loss of power and authority. Please get that. There are so many in the church today who believe that sin and righteousness are allowed to be mixed.

1 Corinthians 10:1-12, reveals examples to us, that we, New Testament believers, may overcome what others could not overcome. We learn to avoid demonic covenants and demonic words. You heard people say things like, "I swear on my mother's grave", and "cross my heart and hope to die". There is no authority to change things for your good in that kind of language. Those type of strongholds are arrogant, because they exalt certain stubborn preferences and desires above the truth of the gospel of Jesus Christ. Just because someone said those particular things while you are listening, does not mean that they are things you should say. Jesus said, *"to take heed what you hear."* In other words, don't ever be an unquestionable listener. Question what you hear before you receive it.

"Your Tongue, Your Future"

As a believer, you've been given the power to receive privileged information. Many times, that privileged information is pressed upon us by the Holy Spirit, who knows all things, and who reveals all things to us that we might be pre-armed for the seasons ahead. It's not just information for seasons ahead, for privileged information can be for the moment. The words that you and I receive through current Kingdom Revelation, will start the process of life above the ordinary in every situation. No one has a choice of whether, or not we will live by words, but we have all been given the choice by which words we will live by. As we stated in the beginning, divine authority causes change to be made by words. In Romans 4:17, it declares calling things that be not as though they were. James 3:2, declares that power lies in consistency. Hebrews 3, declares that Jesus is High Priest of our words. So just from these Scriptures we can see that changes made from the power of words. If you want life, then start declaring life. If you want your marriage to grow stronger, then speak words that cover any weakness. If you want your future to be a success, start declaring the revelations that you are receiving as you read these divine chapters. Set up a memorial on your tongue, that declares that the things that you receive belong to you and your children forever. If you believe you must speak, because what I'm in agreement with I must become one with. Proverbs 12:18 says, *"that the tongue of the wise is health."* So, if I want greater health, I have got to use a wiser tongue. Proverbs 13:2-3 says, *"that a man should eat good by the fruit of his mouth."* The fruit of the tree is known as the wealth of the tree. What wealth is rolling out of your mouth? Is it the wealth of being able to afford a new home? Is it the wealth of having a great life, a successful future? Your tongue has a lot to do with how things turn out in life. Philemon 6 says, *"that the communication of thy faith may become effectual, by the acknowledging of every good thing which is in you in Christ Jesus."* In other words, your faith must be active, energetic, and at work in every situation, saying what the Bible says about you. Jesus is the mind of God encapsulated in flesh. Jesus is God's will for us, so repeat God's will for yourself over and over until you overcome. Psalms 89:34, *"My covenant will I not break, nor alter the thing that is gone out of my lips."* Shows you the work of our faith filled, godly tongue in authority. Success in life through revelations will help tremendously as you pursue the opportunities of a Godly life before heaven and earth.

CHAPTER EIGHT

"The Revelation of Divine Inheritance"

Divine inheritance, represents the provision, protection and well-being of every believer, ordained by the God of justice, for the welfare and establishment of His covenant. Praise God! In Genesis 22:16-18, we see our inheritance that was promised by Almighty God. It is written, and it cannot be annulled or broken. *"God is not a man that he should lie, nor the son of man that he should repent,"* as is recorded in Numbers 23:19. To establish His covenant in the earth, spiritual terrains will have to be rearranged. When we say spiritual terrains, we are not just talking about dealing with neighborhoods, nations, or cultures. A lot of rearranging spiritual terrain takes place in our hearts. To establish His covenant, God's word says, that He would need wealthy people. Covenant means, that He is committed to us and our generation to come, and so the renewing of the mind is an absolute must to walk in divine inheritance. Poor people can give, but not at the level of opportunity that wealthy people can. It takes more people under the umbrella of being poor, to give a certain amount, that will only take a few wealthy people to give. Jesus said, *"that we would have the poor with us always"*, so we don't dismiss poor people, because they are very important for us. For when the poor is given to, it is a loan to Almighty God, and that even with interest added. So, revelations like this one is to help encourage your renewed mind to grab more light and sight into God's will for you. It is never God's will that His people be without or begging as if we do not have the Lord, as our Shepherd. Divine inheritance covers a lot of things, not just monetary things, but every provision for your life. Remember, the definition is about provision, which is ordained by God.

Let's talk a little bit about the rearranging of spiritual terrains within. We should never think we are successful just because we were successful in the world, for the Kingdom success is much greater. Under the worlds umbrella, the heart contained at least 13 defilements, all which were called evil. Now that we are born-again, those traits of the heart have been washed by the blood of Jesus, but the amount of damage upon the flesh that came from the heart, may still have to be dealt with. You may be born-again, but there still may be covetousness in your flesh. You say that is not possible, but your giving to the Kingdom, will always account for faith or unbelief. You may have unbelief embedded in your flesh, which now kicks against you believing to receive the windows of heaven open for you. That principle applies to those of the tithers and members of God's goodness. Every woodlot started from some form of seed that was planted in the ground. The wind may have blown seeds, squirrels may planted seeds, or maybe that half-eaten apple thrown out the car window caused an apple tree to grow. The ground, which represents a heart, will produce in the atmosphere around it, which represents the flesh, things that are imprinted from the heart. Yes, we are born again, but we must renew our minds, which have been imprinted with many things that cause unbelief. Unbelief is always been Satan's way of controlling every institution, including your mind. Proverbs 5:21, reveals to you and me, that Jesus cannot be deceived. His judgments are not based on any natural sense but is pure and truthful. How? He looks into the deep places of our lives and He ponders always. This is why, we study the revealed Word, so that any spiritual terrain may be rearranged to fit God's will. In 2 Corinthians 10:5, it gives us a directive to *"cast down imaginations and every high thing that exalts itself against the knowledge of God and bringing into captivity every thought to the obedience of Christ."* The scripture is sharing with us how to change spiritual terrain within. Most of us know how to deal with spiritual terrain on the outside, yet the income and resources of the local ministries of God suffer at the hands of the enemy, because the spiritual terrain within most people is never changed. We read that God is committed to us and to our generations, so we must be committed to Him.

If you have ever studied world history, you note that curses are very real. They have weakened people, and nations, for defeat. Throughout history, Bible history included, we see generations suffering from the effects of different types of curses. You have seen people weakened in families by certain calamities that seem to follow generation after generation. Sometimes, even though families know that something is wrong, they cannot put their finger on it to identify it. They look for a carnal excuse, but there are none. The truth is, there is a curse upon that family, culture or nation, that is weakening it for destruction. Proverbs 26:2 says, *"that a curse causeless shall not come."* In other words, we would say today that something caused that thing to happen that we don't know about. From Genesis through Revelation, the blood has been the lifting agent that causes curses to be removed. Genesis 8:20-21 records, *"that when the blood was placed upon the altar, God received it, and spoke never to bring a curse again upon the ground for man's sake."* Today you and I live by the power of the blood of Jesus, which causes all curses to lose the legality of function against us. Galatians 3:13-14 declares, *"that the blood of Jesus has freed us and our inheritance from the jaws of a curse."* You must get this. The blood of Jesus freed us from the master of sin, for we were slaves to sin. Now we are slaves to righteousness, because we have our new master, praise God. But our inheritance that was bound in the palace of a strongman, has been taken and distributed to each and every believer. It has been set aside for us to function in and through, that God's covenant might be established upon the earth. Matthew 12:29 says this, *"Or else how can one enter into a strong man's house, and spoil his goods, except to first bind the strong man? And then he will spoil his house."* This is Jesus declaring His victory over the enemy and releasing our inheritance that was bound by sin and the curse of Adam's disobedience.

It is a powerful thing to understand that God wants you so blessed that you can be envied. It is a great revelation to know that even though I am not where I should be in resources, that God's Word cannot be annulled, and He will help me fulfill that Word. When reading Peter's letter to the church, 2 Peter 1:3-11, the Holy Spirit is revealing that carnal power has nothing to do with your inheritance. Again, carnal power, which the world lives by, has nothing to do with you being an heir of God, and a joint heir with Christ Jesus. Peter says here, *"that according as his divine power has given unto us all things that pertain unto life and godliness, through the knowledge of him that have called us to glory and virtue. Whereby are given unto us exceeding great and precious promises; that by these you might be partakers of the divine nature, having escaped the corruption that is in the world through lust."* You can read the rest of the Scriptures to fix your mind on light and sight, the more light, the more sight; the more sight, the more clarity; the more clarity, the better choosing; and the better choosing, the better life. That's what these revelations are for, you and your family having a better life. Scriptures are full of types and symbols that men trust in, but as a believer, you and I must trust the divine power that is given us the welfare of a divine inheritance. Now that we know that our inheritance has nothing to do with our carnal thinking, let us stretch forth and lay hold of the Scriptures, and fill our hearts with divine order that we may have success in life.

CHAPTER NINE

"The Revelation
of Divine Inheritance"
Part 2

I n continuing with this revelation, we can never leave out how to rearrange the spiritual terrains. There are times when we have to do warfare, and then there are times where we have to use divine strategies. Wisdom is the most important factor in divine strategies, and it is important to remember that there are more ways to get to a particular place than maybe we think. You can drive a car to DC, or you can ride a bike. We simply say choose the best strategy, or warfare if necessary, to get you to the place of blessing. We have always taught men and women to tithe, because tithing declares that we believe Jesus is alive. Now if you are not a tither, it may be one of those situations that we talked about in an earlier chapter. Unbelief does not go away, because you go to church, unbelief is a spiritual terrain that must be removed and rearranged. Hebrews 7:8, places you and I into a point of contact with our High Priest, Jesus Christ. It connects us with the highest ministry of intercession there is, that through Jesus Christ, the Son in whom God is well pleased, who now connects us to the Melchizedek's Priesthood. This connection allows us to draw from the One who has an endless life. Here is some background to help you understand the position that Jesus holds now, which gives us privilege to connect to His endless life. In Mark 9:2-8, Jesus is transfigured before His disciples on a chosen mountain. Then two other Bible characters show up, namely Moses and Elijah. Moses and Elijah are from different generations in the history of the Bible, and yet these two, who show that God is the God of the living, meet with Jesus and have a conversation about Jesus finishing His work in Jerusalem. Moses is known as the great intercessor, for he interceded for Israel when God wanted to destroy them. Elijah is known as the great reformer, for he bought Reformation to Israel, fathers to sons and sons to fathers. When Peter spoke up and said, *"let us build three tabernacles, one for Jesus, one for Moses, and one for Elijah, God the father spoke from a cloud and said, this is my son in whom I am well please, hear him."* From the time of Jesus' resurrection and ascension, Jesus has taken on all three dimensions, the Intercessor, the Reformer, the Blesser. All are within the Melchizedek Priesthood. If I know that I am an heir (Romans 8:17), then following principles become very easy for me. It is only when we do not know who we are that we cannot declare who we are to be.

Scripture has declared that there is a wealth transfer for those who are joint heirs with Christ Jesus. James 5:1-4 declares, the treasures have been heaped up for the last days, and those treasures will be dispersed to the godly. Ecclesiastes 2:26 says this, *"for God giveth to a man that is good in his sight wisdom, and knowledge, and joy; but to the sinner he giveth travail, to gather and to heap up, that he may give to him that is good before God".* John 10:10 reveals, *"that Jesus came that we might have life above the ordinary."* What is ordinary? Toil and worry, frustration and lack, poverty and want, and never ever having enough to say you have enough. Think about this for just a moment. When you magnify an object, you enlarge it so that you can better understand. When subjects such as these are magnified, you enlarge your awareness of them, you understand them better, and now you can apply them. That's what these teachings are all about. Deuteronomy 29:29, still states that *"the things that are revealed to us belong to us and to our children, that we may do all the law."* In other words, the light and sight of revelations, give you understanding that they may be applied in your life. Without understanding, it does not matter what the subject might be, you will never be able to apply it to your life with success.

The value of any promise is proportionate to the authority of the one who gives it. As the Holy Spirit has given us promises of increase, retribution, and paybacks, we should take these to heart, knowing that this is God's will for us. As the author and the finisher of our faith, Jesus is personally involved in us finishing with a fruitful life. You cannot hear right when there are problems in the heart.Matthew 26:59-67, gives us a picture as plain as the light of day, that in their hearts, the religious leaders of that day had already planned to kill Jesus no matter what He said. Hearing and heart connection are vitally important to knowing you have a divine inheritance. If all you listen to are others groans of complaints, the negative strategies to manipulate, or the roars of carnal minds filling the atmosphere with defeating words, it will be very hard for you to obtain a revelation of your inheritance in Christ Jesus. 1 Peter 3:9-12 says, *"that we are to not render evil for evil or railing for railing; but contrariwise blessing; knowing that you are thereunto called, that you should inherit a blessing."* We could do a little self-examination right here and ask ourselves a question or two. Do we have desire to establish God's covenant in the earth? Can we make a quality decision to act on the word immediately? Do we have enough determination to receive our inheritance? The pages of this book cannot answer those questions for you, because this book cannot make the choice for you no matter how much information it holds. You have to choose life or death. You have to choose whether you are going to be mediocre, or whether you are going to aim for remarkable. You have to choose whether your family will be transformed into their inheritance or whether they will work for carnal increase, which is always temporary. As you dig deeper into the spiritual terrain of your heart, do not allow any unbelief to remain. Pull it up by the root and throw it away from you, as far as, you possibly can. Set your mind in righteousness, and do not allow a problem to become the biggest thing in your life. Worrying about things and struggling with it will not change a thing. Choose the thoughts of God and cast down thoughts that come against the revealed Word of God. Do what you have learned through Scripture, and never think that a small beginning is the end of things. For even a mustard seed can grow to the place that it becomes a tree. You will perpetuate whatever is first in your life, and if the Word of God is first, then your life will have the success that only God can write.

"Standing Rules for Victory"

Holdfast to the absolute Lordship of Jesus. He is Lord over all things, and remember, He can turn your mistakes into blessings. Continually confessing the Scriptures on wealth transfers, inheritances, paybacks and reimbursements. The Word of God is filled with such promising words that bring divine order to those spiritual terrains in our life that need to be filled. Make declarations of how Jesus is made unto you, wisdom, righteousness, sanctification and redemption. Remind yourself every day, that provision from the Kingdom of God can come in many different ways. Never box God into an experience that you had, or that someone else had. Experiences in life change as fast as the wind blows. One experience, positive or negative, could have been caused by you. That same experience could later on be caused by other people. So, we never put God in a box, because He is the Lord our Shepherd, He leads, and we follow. God is always fair in His dealings, for He has given clear instruction of how to live godly lives, which is the foundation for all prosperity. When we obediently follow His ways, He will take care of us and bless us. Always have faith in your faith. Always have faith in what Jesus has done for you, regardless of what the world may claim you to be. You are not poor, you are rich. You are not the tail; you are the head.

CHAPTER TEN

"The Revelation of Divine Movement"

I n receiving and understanding revelations, we are able to live in the
power that others are not touching. We pull the revealed things into our life,
which may remain secrets to other people throughout our lifetime. Revelation
is more powerful than miracles, signs, and wonders. Why? Because, it changes
our minds and the way we think about ourselves. We become empowered to
know things that set us free. John 8:31-32 records Jesus saying these words, *"If
you continue in my word, then are you my disciples indeed. And you shall know
the truth, and the truth shall make you free."* This is why revelation knowledge is
so powerful to us. There are spiritual terrains in our life, sometimes called paradigms, that only the Word of God can free us from. Inside this chapter of Divine
movement, we will position ourselves for divine visitations. In Genesis 1:2, we
see the Spirit of God moved and brought order to an environment in chaos. The
Holy Spirit is never silent or motionless, for He moves, speaks, enables, and He
releases power to change people and circumstances. Even before the birthing of
our Lord Jesus Christ, Gabriel's response to Mary was that when the Holy Spirit
comes, power comes to make things, to change things, and to make things right.
When the spiritual manifestations of the Holy Spirit are loosed among God's
people, they ignite a fire, that exposes sin, drives out darkness, sets people free,

and brings revelation knowledge that gives light and sight. Today, the Holy Spirit is moving in your life. Right now, the Holy Spirit is opening up pathways for you to have a new future. You have come this far in reading about revelations, and the one who gives those revelations is connected to you right now. The Holy Spirit is releasing power in your life right now to change the standard of your future. There are things that you have yet to pray about, that He is working on right now. There are desires that you will have next year, that are different than desires you have today, all because He is working and releasing a greatness on you. You're favored by God, always know that He's working all things for your good.

Acts 10:38 declares, *"how God anointed Jesus, with the Holy Ghost and power, who went about doing good, healing all who were oppressed of the devil."* The book of Acts makes it clear that when the Holy Spirit is allowed to move, His moving results in power. Power to change positions, and power to cause progress toward a certain state. When allowed to move, the Holy Spirit will bring forth new seasons and a newness of thinking. When the Holy Spirits' power is released, that divine power unleashes the supernatural that does what the human mind and natural talent could never do. There are works that we could never achieve without the working of the Holy Spirit. We see how Jesus went about doing good, but that good done was accompanied by the Holy Spirit. How do you feed thousands of men and women with a few loaves of bread and fish? Only by the divine presence and demonstration of power through the Holy Spirit. The revelation that Jesus worked through from the Holy Spirit's mind bore victory after victory with His encounters of the needs of others. How do you cast out a legion of demons that was tormenting a man's life? By the finger of God, the Holy Spirit. How can people just touching the border of Jesus' garments become whole? By the indwelling presence of the Holy Spirit. Divine movement, by the Scriptures that we read, is God's ability to accelerate whatever measure of resource that is needed at the time. Because, there is no time in God's power, God's faith always acts in the spirit of the future, not the past. Divine motion by the Holy Spirit supersedes the law of time. Time is progressive, moment by moment, day by day, and year by year. But, divine motion by the Holy Spirit is not governed by what we know as time but is moved by faith. All of us know that faith is now. *"Now faith is the substance of things hoped for, the evidence of things not seen."*

God's ability to accelerate any substance, has been shown through Jesus turning water into wine. In the natural, developing wine is a process. In the natural, there are many ingredients that need to be added to the fruit, to produce what is known as wine. Jesus never went through the process, or the ingredients added, to make wine. His spoken word, which was always governed by the power the Holy Spirit, turned water into wine. The acceleration process was very short and very sure. Fill the pots and draw out. You cannot get much faster than that. Fill the pots required a little effort on the part of the servants, and draw out and give to the governor, required a little more effort, but that's it. The final product was wine that tasted better than the wine that man had processed. The product of the Holy Spirit working is always going to be better than the work of man's hands. Study John 2:1-11, as you are digging deeper. The healing of eyes, giving sight to the blind, and even giving sight to one that was born blind, are all under the workings of the Holy Spirit. The pattern that Jesus laid out for us, is to draw out the very best resources by the power the Holy Spirit. In Mark 10:46-52, rest a remarkable story of healing blinded eyes. Blind in his eyes but having hearing in his ears, Bartimaeus hears that Jesus is passing by. The cry for mercy will always get Jesus attention, and mercy will open the door for grace. Divine motion healed the blind man and set him in motion to follow Jesus. The revelation of who we see God to be, will create the faith dimension we are able to walk in. The blind man called Jesus the Son of David, which can only be revealed as God in the flesh. This was David's promised son that would rule the kingdom. The blind man upon hearing that it was Jesus, could see Him for who He was. In causing divine movement to take place in our life, we must see God for who He is, not for who people say He is. During that time, some called Jesus all kinds of names, some kind and some unkind. But who he really is matters greatly to one seeking to cause divine movement to take place in their life.

The Book of Acts is a "Book of Patterns". These patterns are set to continue to the end of the church age (Matthew 16:18). We see in the book of Acts that the first deacon core was established by the Holy Spirit's divine movement. Acts 6:8, reveals how the Holy Spirit was moving upon those who were chosen, and great miracles were taking place to progress the church toward a certain state. In Acts 8:5-8, we see the Holy Spirit visibly moving in Samaria. Philip is there preaching, and again we see miracles changing spiritual terrain within the people, and we see the kingdom of darkness falling by the wayside because, of the power and the movement of the Holy Spirit. In Acts 10:44-45, it is recorded that while Peter is speaking, the Holy Spirit begins moving vocally, outwardly and visibly among the hearers. In Acts 19:1-7, we see Paul laying hands on at least 12 men and the Holy Spirit moved on them and they spoke in other tongues and prophesied. Who is moving that causes all the supernatural manifestations to take place? The same Holy Spirit who in the beginning when the world was in a chaotic environment, He moved to bring order by the Word of God. He is still moving today, bringing supernatural motion to cause things to spring forth in new power. As a believer, *"we live under the law of the Spirit of Life in Christ Jesus that set us free from the law of sin and death."* We have God's open hand through the Holy Spirit, that satisfies the desire of every living thing. God has always loved to satisfy His creation with good things, and the divine motion of the Holy Spirit's involvement in our lives will carry us day-to-day to good things. Some, because of religion, theology, or some paradigm, consider that some of the things of the Holy Spirit is working may be by accident. That is not true, because *"Jesus is the author and the finisher of our faith,"* which means He is personally involved in our lives.

When the Israelites approached the first fruits city of Canaan, (which we call the city of Jericho), God told them to march around the city seven times. Even though they did not understand why and even though it seemed crazy, they obeyed. When they obeyed, history has it that those walls went straight down into the ground, giving passage for Israel to go right into the city. It was divine movement under the ground by the Holy Spirit, and it caused victory to take place above ground. You may not see everything the Holy Spirit is doing, it may be underground, but the victory will definitely be yours. Study Joshua chapter 6, for you are in the spirit of digging deeper. In 1 Kings 18:41-45, we have the story of the prophet Elisha telling his servant to go look over the sea seven times. It was not until the seventh time in the final trip that the servant saw the miracle sign that Elijah was praying for. Who created that cloud the size of a man's hand? You got that right, the Holy Spirit. He is the one who brings order to chaos, and at that time the drought was causing chaos. Then, there's Naaman, the mighty commander of the Syrian army. Even though he was a mighty man in the Syrian army, he was also a leper, which would definitely give him a defeating end in life. Elisha, the Prophet of God, told him to dip in the Jordan River seven times. Why seven times? Well, if you study the Bible, you know that seven represents the number of completion. This made Naaman so furious, because it was not how he expected to be healed. But, when finally persuaded by the servant, he trusted and obeyed the word that was given to him, and only dipped seven times in that little old muddy river, he was supernaturally healed. How? Because, the Holy Spirit is not hindered by material resources, but within them, He can use them to accelerate His supernatural resources. We can see from the stories that the Holy Spirit can be moved by childlike, persistent faith, and it is no different today with you. If you use childlike, persistent faith, divine movement will rest upon your circumstances and bring you to new seasons of joy. Just imagine how joyful Naaman was, a grown man walking around with the flesh of a young child. The Holy Spirit does make all things new, because *"all things are possible to him that believe"*. As a believer, remain a believer. Let nothing take you away from the blessing of revelation knowledge. Now that you have been with me in these teachings, it's time to act in faith. What you do now, will set the stage for what God does next. James 4:8 tells us, *"to draw near to God, and he will draw near to you."* I call you blessed and highly favored, aim to be remarkable.